Scrap Iron

SCRAP IRON

Mark Jay Brewin Jr.

Mark Jay Brewin Jr.
2 AUGUST 2014
SEWANEE, TN

MATT,

WELL, SHIT, SIR. I CAN'T TELL YOU HOW
THRILLED I AM THAT TO HAVE MET.
WITH HOPE FOR OUR WORDS.

LOVE,
MARK

THE UNIVERSITY OF UTAH PRESS

Salt Lake City

THE AGHA SHAHID ALI PRIZE IN POETRY
Series Editor: Katharine Coles
Advisory Editor: Jacqueline Osherow

The Defiance House Man colophon is a registered trademark
of the University of Utah Press. It is based on a four-foot-tall
Ancient Puebloan pictograph (late PIII) near Glen Canyon, Utah.

17 16 15 14 13   1 2 3 4 5

LIBRARY OF CONGRESS CONTROL NUMBER: 2013933800
CIP data on file with the Library of Congress

Cover image © Mohammed Siraj. Used by permission of the photographer.

CONTENTS

But I believe above all that I wanted to build the palace of my memory, because my memory is my only homeland.

—ANSELM KIEFER

Scrap Iron

Water was always the problem surrounding
our rancher anchored to the low end of the acreage—
rain lurched in, ankle-deep pools filled every dip
in the road, and when shin-high floods overtook
the asphalt bulkhead my father built along
the driveway's sides, he donned his fisherman's rain suit,
shoveled sand along the edge to keep street gutters
from overflowing and making our house an island
in a slump of the farmed plain. Sitting inside
during the downpour, I placed the fact cards
of my Illustrated Wildlife Treasury end to end
on my bedroom floor—mockingbird, *Mimus polyglottos*;
giant deer, *Megaloceros giganteus*—memorized
their countries of origin, their characteristics,
organized and reorganized them, while my brother
shoved army men into the floor vent, their plastic bits
tinging against the ducts like rocks against the tiller.
My sister argued with a toy phone. My mother
mixed kidney beans into the tomato sauce,
sliced pepperoni, made sure to give each of us
the same number of slices and took comfort
in her attention, in the fact that her separate, warring
children were in their own corners, relatively quiet
and needful of her to do the cooking. With the dinner
call, my sister and brother leapt for the table,
but I was still imagining the other side of the world—
great spotted kiwi, *Apteryx haastii*; highland cow,
Bos taurus. My mother tried one last time
to fetch my father, who fought the uphill battle
of rain surges washing away sand, but her voice
sunk in the white noise. She left my brother and sister
to eat their pasta e fagioli, sat beside me on the floor
with more pepperoni wedges, and asked,
Where are you at today? How far out are you?

3

PART I

MILKING THE WASTED LAND

BURNING DOWN THE CAMPER

For seven days my father scavenged the junked camper.
He deveined copper wiring from walls, took sledge hammer,
crowbar, and cat's paw to kitchenette cabinets.
His shunted boot buckled doorjambs. His hands
split sewage lines and salvaged the propane stove top.

For seven days, while dismantling the rank trailer—
wrist deep in the musk of petrified mouse carcasses
and sun-cooked frog bodies, insect shells littered along sills—
he longed for the bonfire's shape: farm crates and splintered rafters,
taproots and runners for kindling. The way it would all blaze.

He tore brass knobs from drawers, screws from lumber.
And after seven days, on his weekend off
from the electric utility, he warehoused the wanted parts
in the garage loft and exchanged his scrap iron cash
for two cases of Milwaukee's Best. He piled the RV shards

in a heap—layering house trash, wire casings,
Styrofoam cooler chunks—and hollered for the family to watch
the flames from bare cable spools in the backyard. My mother,
cradling my infant brother, said no, but my sister and I
scrambled beyond the back porch and bobbled around the pit,

waved sunflower stalks like wands over the tattered flames,
chanted gibberish incantations, and with each *Abracadabra!*
our father would chuck empties into the glowing center.
Raking the coals with a bean stake, he stammered facts:
that the worst hell glow is not orange, but white;

that liquefied dinosaurs filled our minivan's gas tank;
that—if we wanted—we could spit on the blistering steel
and watch the dribble vanish, so long as we didn't get too close.
So, we mustered saliva, hocked as much as children could, laughed.
But our father, with other plans for pleasing his audience,

stumbled from the shed, kicking sandbox toys and Wiffle Ball bats
to where we sat and promised us we would see magic.
He moved a plastic alligator closer to the heat, until
an inch away, its jaws melted, eyebrows and paws puddled
on the bare earth, and we wanted more. Wads of Sunday circulars

flared green, burning gas station coffee cups gave off a pitch smoke.
Window screens shriveled and glass panes burst.
Two-liter cola bottles, after a flash from the garden hose,
collapsed in on themselves as if ghost wrung. He used
words like *vacuum* and *pressure*. They meant nothing.

By bedtime, all that remained were more beer cans and rubble
coughing up ash, embers giving way to the match heads of stars.
A night dirge. The pucker and fizz of singed wreck.
My mother called for my sister and me to come in,
but my father—enjoying his dawdling children—yelled back

that we were just fine so long as he could stand.
Words turned to marbles in his mouth. The way he spoke

our names, a muttered hex. His guttural song
kept us awake, cursing the power plant and its graveyard shift,
as he entertained his kids with a homemade sacrifice of shrubs,

mowed grass, crumbling shed roof and front deck cross beams.
The knot and grain of stubble around his chin.
The stock and rings of work callusing his hands and fingers.
A shit camper. Hulk and debris rescued from house repairs
and fix-it jobs, good for one last thing: the mystical.

The power in anything that will burn.

JERSEY DEVIL

Whenever the ruddy dusk swallows the sandwash and barrens,
children fed on devil stories tramp the woods' footpaths
shouldering branches whittled to spears and prowl
the rock shore, wade into bog shoals and back—legs stained
from the creek ore and muck. From rickety forts,
they map and raid the scrubland. They palm knives,
scour the tree line and timber shanties, ramble home
toting their marsh-blackened boots. The children peek
through curtain gaps during summer downpours,
play lookout from the covered porch—this is how they keep
the family dog from slaughter. They wrestle the stream-
snagged lure with the thought: *it's him*. The wild thing
that snakes along the crooked river as the brave

plunge from the dock ledge into rusty, cedar water.
The shadow that buries its hoof trail under pine needles

skirting abandoned duck blinds. The savage who loses
its wing scrape and forked tail in the wind-churned oak boughs.
And when night paws at the window, the light-empty bedroom
is so much like the creature's blackjack lair, dreams flash
the mud-padded fur coarse as bark, wild fangs like a jaw of briars.
Mothers and fathers wake at the sound of their own
sharp gasps, bawl and whine that the cursed son hunts for them.
The children light house lamps at the same black hour,
sweet-talk and shoo away the wicked one. They stare beyond
the glass pane and drapes, the yard fence like a band of teeth,
and wonder if they are already tucked in the beast's belly.

HIS GRANDMOTHER AS A WIND CHIME

For Julia Brewin, August 29, 1928–September 1, 2006

His grandmother can't help dragging her kidney-
colored housecoat on the Dalmatian shag carpet,
her short legs onion skinned, her hair a shrub

thinning in fall. She can't help the army of candles
on her marble cake, the bruises, needle pricks,
and scars on her fingers, or that she passes away

in her sleep three days after her birthday, her year-old
grandson, crying, crawling head first into a coffee table
as his parents empty hangers and closets,

trash jars of potpourri from the pink and green bathrooms,
unhook and pack up the prized wind chimes
that clanged by the side door where she'd sit and clean

cornsilk from cobs of Silver Queen and Jersey Sweet.
The old house sells, and the tinny clamber of chimes sings
in a new kitchen as the grandson mouths words and sounds

from his high chair, his mother baby talking to him,
"Hear that, honey? That's Mom-mom talking to you.
Say 'Hi, Mom-mom!'" By the time the grandson

is naming objects—laundry bins and diaper boxes—
his parents tuck him in his crib, and years later, ask him,
"Did you say goodnight to Mom-mom? Go say

'Goodnight.' Ask her for good dreams." He marches out
of his room, kneels beneath the wind chimes and whispers.
And the grandson believes the raw metal tubes,

the knotted thread and steel loops are the body of his lost
grandmother, believes they croon to him throughout the day,
knell approval at the sight of crayon sketches of a boy

perched beside a wreath of ringing pipes. During art class
at the kindergarten and elementary school, he sculpts
modeling clay into snakes and little hammers,

comes home to a snack of grapes, a backdrop of soft gongs
and tolls, his mother declaring, "There she goes
again! I swear your grandmother only makes a peep

when you're here!" He gets dropped off
at the middle school early so he can raise the state flag
outside the main office, stays after for band practice

where he plays the vibraphone and sits first chair. At night,
he has dreams of swinging, strings and cords hugging him,
his limbs hollow rods, his mouth a ringing bell.

SCRAP IRON

We hunted for steel along flat-bottom train rails—glass
        blanketing the gravel track bed like chicken feed,
jimson weed between creosote-steeped timbers—
        picked over buckled trailers and garbage stacks:
cracked pump heads, mower blades, band saws rusted mid-cut.
        The clang of spikes and bolt heads lobbed into a bucket
was a lesson he taught me in milking the wasted land.

Those days were oil tanks chain-dragged home
        on the city road, rotting doors burnt in our backyard
so that I could rake the hinges and metal from the ash.
        Those days were broken appliances I held down
while he tore off the unwanted plastic and rubber gaskets.

Evenings, my father exhausted the fridge's thirty-rack
        one beer at a time and reviewed the math of cents-per-pound
as I swatted away wasps that hummed from nests
        in the trashed air conditioner's A-coil, and in and out
of the mouths of empties I crumpled under my heel.
        I refastened the flapping sole of my hand-me-down boots
with screws plundered from a pool scrubber head.
        The tiny spirals shined in my palm like loose change.

His long weekends off and the truck bed crammed full,
        balanced and roped, we drove across town to cash in.

"Don't let them see you when we get weighed on the drive in,"
            he warned me, balled below the glove box, hiding under
work shirts and newspapers, palms cupped over my mouth
            masking my breathing until we made the junkyard's jagged heap.

Knowing that we'd make an extra forty-five bucks if I
            wasn't in the truck during weigh out, I snuck
my way around the hissing hydraulic compactors, hustled past
            the growling machines and grease-tanned forklift drivers.
I kept my hands in my pockets and thought about what was worse:
            if one of the dump workers found me, or the look on my father's
face if they did—how if I didn't get caught, my body
            was an extra hundred and twenty-some pounds of scrap.

BIVALVE, CUMBERLAND COUNTY

It is hunger they cast from the docks, a long pang
that keeps cattailed mudflats barren and ravages
the mucky shoreline of booming mollusk beds
and concrete-block shucking houses. It is
hunger that creeps up the Maurice River's forking
inlets and backwater channels, a parasite
that swallows oyster crops and grounds boat captains,
a germ that empties nets and poisons canals.
This is how the brackish wetlands became scarred
with salt-rotted wharfs and crumbling fishing shacks
and lost the clack song of shells, split and stacked,
of tin cans brimming with briny hearts. Even now,
there is the ebbing wake against gull-soiled
pilings, a rude wishbone for rich tides
and fresh catches. Each winter, when the marsh
is dusted, when the currents ferry ice shards,
the bolted houses and gaunt locals wait
for a harsh cold that will nearly break them,
quiet the bay, leave them with the faint memory
of warmth, clutching not pearls or handouts,
but the slim chance in the spring to work for oysters.

ON PEELING SKIN

Evening sun held the horizon
    like a blood-flushed palm.
It set and cut through curtain gaps,
    cast light tracks through the kitchen
and den. After mowing the yard and field,
    skirting grass clippings
around raspberry cones, burning
    dead shrubs and cracked porch lattice,
my father came in from his long day
    of summer work—his dinner plate
already made and placed in the microwave.
    First, the patchy kiss
from thumbing open the tab of his beer.
    Next, the TV channel
switched from *Unsolved Mysteries* to *Night Court*.
    He washed his hands after eating,
knocked off his boots, and rested facedown
    on the living room floor.
And finally, when the windows were slid open—
    our house flooded
with night breeze and bug chirp—my father
    gave the go-ahead. My brother and sister
and I huddled around his bare,
    baked shoulders and laid

our small, cool hands on his still-warm back,
       and began stripping off
flakes of sunburned skin. We had little contests
       to see who could pull
the largest piece, the best shape. We tended
       him as if we could peel
the mark of hard work from his body.

MIDNIGHT SHIFT

I knew what the power plant kept from the house. Two in the morning, my mother would nudge me awake and carry me on her hip into the master bedroom. My father's side of the mattress looked bare. The alarm's red numbers reflected off the mirror and flashed the opposite wall, and the turn-dial television blinked in the corner. A preacher was on channel five, waving a green handkerchief with gold trim. He promised the swatches of material cured arthritis and sickness, healed wounds and brought money to a broken home. His whoops kept me up though my mother curled over on her side and slept, a man's voice humming through the house. I got up to switch on the ceiling fan, crawled to the knob, searched the stations but settled back on the preacher. It looked like a flood had slicked back his hair. If I had enough cord to walk the telephone receiver over and stand beside the screen, I'd like to think I would have called my father to ask him if he lit the lamps in that church. If I had enough cord, I'd like to think I would have dialed the number to have the holy man pray for my father's machine-crushed hands, his missing fingers.

OUR LADY OF MOUNT CARMEL

Blessed Saint, my great-grandfather spoke of you
on the odd Saturdays he babysat me—
under the soggy peanut shell of his skin, muscles
soured and nerves unlinked like the backyard swing's chain,
hands and legs petrified, near useless from Lou Gehrig's disease.

He had me play parent and wipe out ashtrays,
boost him up plywood ramps and switch channels.
When I finished tearing open wrappers to feed him candy,
he talked about how he kept the porch flowerbox.
When I asked him how come he got to camp out, year round,
on the sleeper sofa by the television in the den,

he praised your church festival: a week
of cooked sausage, grease dripping from sandwich buns,
funhouses and carnival rides sticky from spilled beer.
A throng of kneelers at candled shrines.
A feast day of hangovers and rosaries for sale.

Our Lady of Mount Carmel, my great-grandfather's wheelchair
towed a bladder of tubes and plastic.
Between playing with bookends in the shape of reading monks
and rearranging magnets on the refrigerator door,
I smacked the catheter as if it were a watery punching bag,
sang nursery rhymes to the clatter of loose boards

below the rolling tire tread. Holy Mother,
you once bestowed blessings and safe passage to immigrants
en route to blueberry orchards, and my great-grandfather's mind
is a stranger in the foreign landscape of his body.
Please, wheel him one last time between the Sicilian pastry vendors

and Sons of Italy clambake stand, into St. Joseph's Parish
to your painted image. Let him pray for another chance
to weed his tomato garden. Let him have his funnel cake supper,
a paper plate of long hot peppers. Virgin Mary,
tame his wild bed of morning glories by the pump spigot.
Carry his brittle husk upstairs to a bed where he hasn't slept in years.

THE PECKING ORDER

I

Steps from the chain-link fence, us schoolboys
shoved each other below the schoolyard magnolia.
We pelted the runs of pale flowers
spotting the stocky limbs, used fallen pine cones
and rocks and lumps of loose asphalt
to drop the tree's stubby seed pods.
We split the gathered shells and pocketed
the red kernels hidden inside
like lost marbles. No one asked why we did it,
no one counted the split husks.
We just followed the play some boy started:
called each other *gay*, threw elbows,
and fought because someone else did.
We tried to seem bigger than we actually were.
We forgot what the teachers said
and stomped through the magnolia blossoms
scattered among the knobby roots like birdseed.

II

Whether they remember or are curious again, C. G. and Ruth Byrd

      ask Victor Recondo about how he knows Jerry Vines.
"We're brothers," he says. "That's right—you're brothers," they respond.
They do this because the whole retirement home whispers about this,
and is restless with the answer.

      The Byrds, like every other resident, believe the pair is
something like a married couple; they search Victor for his "brother's"
family looks, but find none. They grapple the queer lisp of his
Spanish tongue against Jerry's Manhattan-drawl, they compliment his
diamond-freckled pinky rings. They inquire, "We hear Jerry

      gets cafeteria takeaway for the both of you, carries it back in a basket."
"Jerry brings me a picnic dinner every day," Victor returns. The Byrds
and the retirement home are left with this, whether or not they are
restless. Victor tells them they are brothers,

      and it is different from the salad days. Victor and Jerry take
      the questions and whispering tenets with their picnic dinner.

III

This is what I heard of it. Run off the road, my uncle's
boyfriend in the drainage gulley, barely breathing, the officer

parked beside the curled guard rail and muddied ditch.
My Uncle Darren held Carlos by kneeling behind him

and draping his arms across his heaving chest.
This is what the trooper saw.

He called in an ambulance for my uncle's boyfriend.
"Asthma attack," he whispered over his radio to the dispatcher,

said he suspected alcohol or foul play. Carlos
belted to the stretcher, hospital bound—the officer walked

back to the scene, and my uncle ready with questions
and *how-is-he-doing*'s. The trooper fired back

with the sobriety line and tests,
yelling at my sobbing uncle, "Stop it, goddamn it.

You got no right to hear about him. Stop bitching,
you faggot chicken-shit." Tired of his cries,

the officer wrestled my whimpering uncle
into the backseat stepping on shards of windshield

and car pieces sown along the field ditch and soft shoulder.
"I got no choice but to take you with me,"

he said to my uncle. "You brought this on you. You must have been on something."

STANDING IN THE ATLANTIC OCEAN
WITH TESLA'S PIGEON

I'm buttoned up in midnight's jacket, star glow
pinpricking the pitch black. Foam ribbons along the water's edge.
Warped pilings splinter lightning rods. Walking into the ocean,
wavechurn belting my waist, I squint into the six inches
I can see around me and watch the chalky smudge
of the Milky Way lose itself against the flash of a coming storm
tucked up against the horizon. The sea flickers its offering back,

and a smack of jellyfish rises to the surface. A yawn of tentacles.
Umbrellas with no wires. Suddenly plugged-in, the soft bells twinkle on,
a riddle of light doubling as the sky's reflection—bioluminescence.
And as I see them glimmer on like bulbs in streetlight globes,
it must be with an awe not wholly unlike when Nikola Tesla stared
at lampposts erected like bookends on every New York City block
and watched Edison's filaments ignite with *his* alternating current?

Eighty-six and skeletal, still a fine figure in a three-piece pinstripe,
he picked wads of bread crusts out of his pockets, walked up
35th toward 5th Avenue, and sowed dinner crumbs by the curbside
for pigeons. The neat split of his hair down the middle. His ears
perked to neon's buzz and traffic din; energy chugging
through the city's veins set him in a trance. The whole earth
struck him like a tuning fork. In that sounding tone, Tesla remembered

how electricity's pulse felt coursing through his body:
the itch under his skin as he allowed jolting limbs from his coil
to crackle and hum for miles and kindle the flickering tongue
inside of him. The wound copper and pipe—a mushroom cap of metal
pinned over a stem of cords. On the opposite side
of his study, the distant thunder of his sparking machine lit beacons
in his hand, unattached to any gadget. Lifted power from the open air.

Swooping into room 3327 from the nest of leaves and twine
on the window ledge, Tesla's pigeon—the one he said he loved
as a man loves a woman—perched at his feet. Gray wingtips.
Fluorescent body. He believed it spoke through its eyes, beams of light,
powerful, dazzling, greater than any lamp in his laboratory.
He stared into the burning ink-drop pupils and dreamed a whole flock
followed in and alighted, his suite white, a glinting chorus. Their bulbs

like the stars, like the jellyfish circling around me, the lightning blazing
a midpoint in the stretching dark. All of the other details blur together:
constellations curve overhead and roll out in front,
the gleaming blooms beneath, and the stars' watery echo.
I reach into both heavens, my skin aware of itself,
waiting for the arc of electricity from that storm to pierce
my body and flip a switch, spark whatever it is inside of me to flash—

enamel and bone and hair, now phosphorescent. Did Tesla want light
to beam from his eye sockets? Maybe man is enamored
with the sweetness of mirroring the cosmic, and maybe despite how fragile
and broken we are, man is able to glow. I hope there is a morsel
of cinder in all of us. And when every candle wick is snuffed out,
when every light goes cold, I'll blink the only way I know,
the earth's clamoring resonance, my crude refrain lost in the endless pitch.

PALACE DEPRESSION

Mill Road, Vineland, New Jersey

I

What is a Palace Depression?
A mud wasps' hive, craggy and scabbed.
The Eccentric's Gospel.
A catacomb of turret spires, graveyard
of half-sunken rust-scarred cars.
Drove of garbage stalagmites.
George Daynor claimed
that when despair swallowed him
an angel came and bid him erect
"a home—a haven of peace
away from breadlines and all such
depressing phenomena."
God's holy will or just
praise in the Sunday paper.
A tourist relic, little Zion
on an Esso gas station roadmap.
A clay pot of pickled dandelion buds
buried and lost in the frost-capped earth.

II

It was an oddball's vision made flesh—
on a swamp of frog spawn and cedar knees—
from the junk stacked in farm fields,

cracked tractor pistons, bent chassis,
gables fashioned from old fenders,
breezeways and barred bed-frame gates.

The castle was a flowering weed
sprouting from Depression-era shanty towns,
balls of chicken wire ripped off barren coops,

and George fueled on tobacco tins of cigarette
butts, burn barrels, newspaper blankets,
pink slips, crumbs scraped from an iron skillet.

III

This is not just about plugging the aching stomach.
While George made revolving doors of wagon wheels,
cold-stung city folk cleared their throats in soup kitchens:
women mended children's clothes with feed sacks,

men pulled plows with their own backs,
all the while, thumbing the two bits in their pockets,
leaning on yard posts, spying to find which of their
packing pallets had become the sloped roofline.

Hungry and moth eaten, they prayed for a helping hand,
their own angel, while they sat, workless, wishing for work,
watching George pulverize redbrick, mix it with crankcase
motor oil and paint—one by one—the growing castle spires.

IV

Come, meet George Daynor's masterwork,
gawk at the peculiar architect on hand.
Watch him stare into the cracked looking glass.

See how he polishes his earring,
paints his bearded face with cherry lipstick,
mattes the glare on his cheeks with blush.

Witness what he has framed and glued
with a plumb bob and odd tackle—the crawl space
he named the Jersey Devil's Den, the turtle-

shell door, the Knockout Room with its boulder
hung above a chair to bat away troubles.
Leave your quarter at the ticket booth.

V

In the prophet's history is a wealth
of tragedy. He claims he owned
a fortune's worth of Klondike gold
lost in the San Francisco earthquake.
It's an unknowable truth long since
buried like his palace tomb—
half plundered, obscured in the sacred.

In the Eccentric's Gospel, the parable
is tailored to fit whatever we want,
promises that "The only real depression
is a depression of individual ingenuity."

In the postcards and sightseers' snapshots,
radio shows and archived news reels,
the artifacts pen a psalm: a forgotten man's
tinkering mind, an indecipherable blueprint,
how in times of trouble we want a holy figure
ready and waiting to be called.

PART II

VOLLEYING ACROSS THE SHOWERY DARK

SO INTRICATE, SO INCONCEIVABLY COMPLEX

My father made his first irreversible mistake at twenty-three, when he
wedged the index and middle fingers of his left hand in the cogs and gears
of a truck winch, twisted and ripped the digits off just below the joint.
My grandparents each offered a finger of their own as a replacement.

The earth is a story of binding and breaking, and as the continents
shimmied into their sandy shards, Gondwanaland severed New Zealand
from the deserted Australian bulk millennia before mammals ever
touched it—bats the only warm-blooded bodies to naturally reach its limit.

I haven't been able to touch gin since I drank Screaming Purple Jesuses
all night long at a costume party where I dressed as Ernest Hemingway.
I changed the color of my beard with white flour to get that salt-
and-pepper look, and carried a toy shotgun I stuck in my mouth for effect.

My father's second irreversible mistake was me. My mother told him
she was pregnant while he was in the hospital for knee surgery—
I don't know if my mother waited until he wasn't able to run or if it was
coincidental. He is always in and out of hospitals for some reason.

While in New Zealand, I won a chest hair and sideburns competition
during a '70s-themed birthday party at a bar in Milford Sound.
I seem to attract opportunities for costumes and alcohol,
but I climbed a pipeline up a mountain the morning after.

My paternal grandparents argued, I would figure, every day of their
married lives. Even in my dreams, I see them cleaning out the garage
and yelling at each other. After my grandmother died, my grandfather
promoted her to family saint. I don't know why they didn't divorce.

That's not true. My grandfather still knows she was a ball-buster.
He sobs every time he hears "The Jitterbug." My grandmother always
wanted a birdbath erected in the backyard. It never happened. Instead,
bats swooped and picked off moths fluttering around the porch light.

New Zealand is split up into two main islands—the North and South—
which, in my opinion, is how New Jersey should be divided.
Not a fact. Just my thought. I also think Ernest Hemingway is a little
overrated. I usually hate to admit this because he has avid fans.

My father had to relearn how to grip objects with his left hand, the nerves
too sensitive to touch anything. When my mother, at the age of twenty,
first met him, she didn't even notice they were missing. He always
kept his hands balled-up on a table. The lost, hidden in plain sight.

The only trail that runs up the mountainside in Milford Sound
is a hydroelectric pipe that harnesses melting glacial water at the peak
into runoff lines. The city center buzzed from the plant's spinning
generators. I wish my father had been there to explain each part to me.

The Maori—the original island people of New Zealand—have tales
to explain every gorge and rock face in their country. A boy pulled
the islands from the water like a fish. A warrior carved a canoe to row
into the underworld to retrieve his dead father. Heartbreaking. Complex.

My grandmother worked at the telephone company for fifty years.
My grandfather twice retired from Sears Roebuck and Co. Auto Center.

My mother was a cosmetologist at Gullo's Hair Salon. My father
pulled extra shifts at the power plant so I could hike another hemisphere.

I tramped the Kepler Track. I shaved the beard I grew in honor
of my father, into the sideburns and goatee that won me a fifty-dollar tab.
I saw glowworms rouse and jewel gorse blooms along the stone beach.
I lost myself among birds and bats and never wanted to be found.

There is a plant in the New Zealand jungle called Five Finger.
Gin is a bottle of alcohol you won't see in my parents' liquor cabinet.
My father went to Canada when he was a kid. My mother left
the continent on a vacation to Hawaii. I was first in the Indian Ocean.

How will I remember my time there? You can spot my father staring off,
his left hand open and flat on the arm of his easy chair, the other scratching
where his lost fingertips would be—doctors call it phantom pains.
Some things don't grow back. Some things you don't lose a feeling for.

ON THUNDERSTORMS

When you stare into the spring storm and heat lightning,
the flashing vein of electricity, weather's dashing pulse,
you count the distance between you and each bolt the way
your father taught you as he stood at the back door—
measuring time between the spark and rumble: *one*

one-thousand, two one-thousand, three one-thousand.... Each beat,
a mile. Each a footstep stretching across the city
and southern part of the state. And though thunder shook
the house during those nights, though you and your sister
hid under quilts in the living room, gasped a little

with each clap, you wanted your mother to leave the blinds
open so you could watch everything. Now, this gale
hunkering down on the neighborhood, you still gaze
at the horizon, follow the show from the front porch.
Plastic lawn chairs. Beers on an end table. No blanket

to tuck under, but your brother beside you—four inches
taller, younger, left here with your sister when you moved
away to college. And where else should he be? Barely twenty,
he stubs out cigarettes on his arm and takes night classes
to be an EMT. He tells you they call him *Junior*

at the firehouse and gun club. You imagine your brother
bolting hoses to corner hydrants at an accident scene,
examining rifle brands at the New Italy banquet hall,
men your father knows and works with, the fire chief, engineers
at the power plant, paramedics teaching courses at the Vo-Tech—

all calling him *Junior,* though it's you who carries your father's
name like a birthmark, like handwriting: something built in.
You empty the can and pull another pair from the cooler.
Wind whips through the new wisteria buds while rainwater
floods the street. The roar drowns out the peepers

and conversation, so you remember the times your family
hurt each other: how you warned your sister you couldn't
grip the storm-bent screen door she crawled under
to rescue a lost ball and hooked the soft flesh of her knee
on the jagged, metal-capped corner; the way the house rang

with your parents—your father drunk and pacing the back deck,
yelling at your mother that you are his favorite child
because you were named after him, and how she said
nothing, only cried; your brother sobbing on your first semester
holiday home, pleading with you to never come back because,

when you did, no one paid any attention to him. And this is how
sound tails the blinding, momentary dissection of the sky.
How frightening it rings after the real danger. How we give
each other scars. The aluminum gutter buckles
from the downpour and a heavy drip pecks at the porch railing,

holds time with your brother's foot tapping. This storm
and a few drinks is about all you two can share anymore, if you

ever shared anything. A bedroom when you were kids.
A sopping memory of indoor picnics your mother would lay out
on rainy days, your sister's hair braided by candlelight, your hands

hammering out the temper of sibling rivalry. With one quick
strike somewhere downtown, the house lamps kick off
and the rancher fills with chatter, thud of footsteps
coursing through every room, your father barking about dead
sump pumps and the basement already ankle deep.

If he's bucketing the water upstairs and out the back door,
he'll need a hand. If you get up from the chair to help,
your brother will only move to grab a fresh beer and tell you,
You can handle it. The show isn't over yet. The power will return
eventually. Ail the alarm clocks will reset to twelve.

FIELD LESSONS

Dr. D'Amato mused about consciousness and suffering in his office,
        between his engineering lectures,
      apprised parables for me after class hours, once said

that when he thought about his ex-wife,
        he remembered how her second toe
      was longer than the big one. While he told me this

he made tea on a plug-in burner,
        fed his office plants from a Mott's Apple Juice jug,
      adjusted books on shelves, offered me Meher Baba—

how love works, when God speaks,
        how we have not come to teach, but awaken.
      That afternoon twittered on until I wished he had curtains

that better covered the snip of light
        teething through office windows,
      how I wanted to speak up instead of just sitting in a stiff chair,

but he quickly slipped into another story, said:
        three army medics were training in Richmond's
      big hospital, assigned to dress gang wounds,

the run of car wrecks and construction trauma,

surly boys wrist deep in sternums and innards,

patching and sewing. A week in,

the soldiers were paged to resuscitate some grandmother.

The battle went on, paddles charged,

needles emptied, but still she died.

Left to toe-tag the lady, these three decided

to rehearse procedures on the body

(hand-over-hand, neck veins tapped, extra potassium).

During their geriatric wisecracks, grandma woke up—

freckled with sensors, draped in an oxygen mask—

and startled these three green berets who couldn't help but hug her.

They'd patched limbs, but never saved somebody.

My old professor reprised,

wondered out loud if they felt like God,

if they noticed the doctor handing pamphlets to the family

for managing these things—sudden passing

and grief and final arrangements—when all I pondered

was if long second toes can curl, if people can heal.

WORKING FIRST SHIFT
AT THE PROGRESSO SOUPS FACTORY

For summer cash, I answered an ad at a work agency
to fill soup cans for three months and they assured me
that if I'd only *apply* myself, there was a decent chance
at full time employment—*You can really make it, but remember,
it's temporary.* I agreed. In September, I would walk

from this calloused glance at another life into my junior year
of college. Steel pitchforks chipped frozen half-dollars
of carrots from a solid vegetable block and the cavernous belly
of the factory clanged even after the chiseling stopped, or so it seemed,
as the overtime workers breaking before their next shift

took their corners of the lunch room and ate leftover rice
and beans, or bit at the quick of their thumbs or glumly stared
at the television chained to its stand—miniature routines,
habits, self-preserving practices of the body. When they stuffed
their khaki work shirts and ear plugs into their lockers,

climbed into their trucks to go home, still I suspected the rest of their
day would play out like this, mechanical. Empty. In high school,
I tried to imagine what my life would be if I followed my father
and became a ditch digger. Attended trade school
and installed burglar alarms for $2.65 an hour. Eventually

got a job loading coal at the power plant. That first week,
with each buzzer or ingredients order from men
lighting the cooking kettles, I hauled fifty-pound sacks
of dried broth or shoveled pasta onto a conveyor belt and peeked
at a book I kept in my back pocket about the supposed extinction

of the ivory-billed woodpecker. After that, I didn't
read another word until the semester set in. I picked up smoking
simply because I could cross to the other side of the compound
and pace the razor-wired yard, spinning my fictional biography
between drags, a history reserved for the unlucky.

Middle school educated. One of seven children. Petty thief
of snack cakes at the gas station counter. Why lie? I was a white boy
from the other side of town: university taught, middle class,
twenty years old with no rent due and no one else but me
to feed off of my paycheck, me who would leave the packing line

for lines of words. I knew everyone there looked at every other
temp worker as someone who could pinch their benefits,
their paycheck, their tin-foiled carnitas in the communal fridge.
Every morning, five a.m., they pinned the labor requisition
beside the punch clock, how many shoulders and hands they needed.

Four for towing pallets. Twelve for sterilizing the boiling pots.
A note penned in the bottom margin—*Send the rest home*.
Every morning, there I was, donning my hardhat and reporting in.
The factory still must have seemed like a machinated version
of an Old Testament enslavement to the workers

who made six dollars an hour inspecting labels glued to every can.
When the foremen said *Order up*, all of us felt the strain.

Palm blisters, back braces. Some shifts we hoped they wouldn't
have enough assignments so we could park at the bodega
on Chestnut Avenue. Those three months were a lifetime—

whether it was the persona I created, the rise and fall
of a species of woodpecker in the book I carried, the stuck note
of the fluorescent bulbs' deafening hum, or how the lighting
in the factory never changed. Yellow lanes marked out where
you could and couldn't move, no straight path from one side

to the other. If you asked me to map out the facility,
I could sketch every nook and staircase, but don't ask me
to name any of the men I borrowed lighters from, the men
to whom I gave my cigarettes at the close of August,
who I told I had to quit. The ones who sucked on the cold beans

they bucketed and weighted for each recipe. Who hacked phlegm
into the lavatory floor drain, penned women's body parts
into the *Daily*'s crossword squares. By September, their names
were lost in my vocabulary, as lost as men who sometimes gazed into
the vending machines as if this were their only occasion for options.

THE ISLAND MEDITATIONS

Dew-matted mornings, I woke to my father
coming home from his midnight shift
of measuring kilowatt-hours, of blocked coal feeds
and overtime. I woke to him by the sink basin
washing the slick glove of oil off his work-swollen knuckles
and fingers, the coffeemaker's huff and purr
just over the hissing faucet. Two black cups.
Eventually he asked if I wanted eggs, *how many?*
He halved shells and whisked the yolks in a bowl.
Once plates were washed and put away,
the garage doors opened, again, he laced up his boots
and trudged outside. Spying from the dining room window,
from my heap of school papers and book pages
I watched him drag the tractor's discs,
how the hitched grater box ate away at the backyard mound
of fill dirt. In my notes from the week's geology lessons,
there was the story of rocks—New England
and the British Isles formed from the same stock,
the same limestone and shale my father kicked up
in the yard, the same stone walls stretching Rhode Island
and Ireland. New Jersey was named for the largest
Channel Island. Edinburgh Castle is stacked on top
of a volcanic formation. The facts stuck upon themselves
and forged a landscape. One of boulder fences

spanning farmland, one where another version of my father—
at that same exact moment—also flattened soil
into the low spots of his yard to keep the threat at bay,
of water closing in around him, where another boy
understood the rough turf he grew up on
a bit more, another boy who found worthwhile land elsewhere.
The clang of rocks against the plow. The ringing in my ears.

[○]

Little scissor-snip scars the length of her fingers.
Her small trimmers unused and ungreased
since the last time she cut hair at the salon.
Her simple questions while she cleaned up my neck
day before I left for New Zealand, "How many
hours difference is it between there and here? Do you want
me to pack your suitcase for you?" And when I said
I'd already loaded everything in my duffle
and canvas book bag, she wondered if she
could look over how I'd arranged my clothes—
"I hope your shirts aren't wrinkled"—despite the fact
she'd already asked twice and I'd twice answered.
The clippers plucked out a hair behind my ear,
as if on cue, and she explained, "I forgot. I'm sorry."
At nearly my age, my mother learned of the delicate
handling mandatory for an infant. She never wanted
to attend college. There were cosmetology classes
when we three kids had full days at school,
and for four years, four days a week she loved it.
I don't know what caused her to leave work
behind. Darwin was an explorer in the sense that
he wanted answers. Not to scale new lands,
but to know them better. Though I'm no pioneer,
I'm still the first in my family to leave
the country, the East Coast, the state. My mother
gone quiet, I said to her, *From Nothingness,*
the Maori believe, came the whole beginning. The earth
and sky were the mother and father, all their kids
were the different elements. You should read the creation story.
They're a people that hopped in their canoes and sailed
beyond their known world. How do you do that?
She told me I was raising my chin, to look down

so she could check the neckline and finish up—
"The lights in here are giving me a headache." Out the window,
the afternoon was gray, and though only home
for the last week, I couldn't think back to a winter
when it wasn't. Worried she would lose her grip
on the comb and scissors, she asked me
to put everything away, so she could lie down.
I should have told her before she went to her room
that despite Darwin's musings on the variety of species
on their solitary islands, on common descent,
he was still buried at Westminster Abbey.
He knew exactly what to say, how to say it,
the keenest way to present his findings and theory—
not once did he mention evolution, only promised
that "light would be thrown" on man's origins
and history. Instead, I checked my luggage,
the last thing she wanted was me forgetting anything.

[○]

"So, tell me, what's it like over there? Tell me all about it."
and my sister goes on and on, minutes borrowed
and bought on a phone card, each echo over the wire
traversing the time zones' invisible borders.
I want to tell her all about the strange mutations
that happen when populations grow isolated,
the magical effect on evolution that islands have,
that otherwise vanish. On these sandy experimental
grounds are the published almanacs of vicariance:
across the north and south islands, colonies
of birds, flightless kiwis combing the underbrush,
the fables of great eagles, giant moas twelve feet tall,
three-toed, carnivorous, hunting tribal men,
women, and children. And more than what is here:
the dwarf elephants of Malta, the enigmatic platypus
paddling the rivers of Australia and Tasmania.
From the rocky clay of Flores, they have uncovered
a real hobbit. In the caves of Palau, are bones,
fragments of skeletons, whole skulls, pygmy,
and it is this, more than anything, I should
tell her, that on the whole of Ireland, you won't
find a snake, and there are stories for this.
In New Zealand, the Maori still fear the Taniwha,
reroute whole highways so as not to disturb its haunt.
Each year, our brother changes his mind about
the profession he wants—classes to be an EMT,
construction work, and now he's opted for
our father's trade, says it's fascinated him all along,
and I hope this is true. Even she, for so long,
studied music, was fluent in a language I could never
grasp, yet she hasn't played trumpet in years. This is what
I understand about evolution, survival: that organisms

divided by a terrestrial barrier alter into a unique species.
Every island I've wandered, the inhabitants are more
of the same, maybe their voice a bit more nasal,
their customs no stranger than ours. But there is
nothing I can muster, no way to explain any of this
over the phone's receiver, except the simple, *It's grand
over here, perfect almost. If only you could see it. I can't tell you
how nice it is to be some place so very different from home.*

[∘]

The way I was raised, *ignorant* only meant *rude*,
not lacking knowledge. Trawling the shallows,
lunar-bruised and reed-thin, the water's ebb and flow
exhuming the sands' buried omens of sharks' teeth,
the scuttle legs of horseshoe crabs torn apart
in the surf, my brother remarks how ignorant his friend was
to not get him another handle of rum
after he knocked it over. Off work, at home
with nothing else to do on a midweek night, we want
the salt air, the blinking radio towers along Corson's Inlet,
the sirens of ambulances volleying across the showery dark
beyond the toll bridge, the Philly blunts we try to light
against the wind while we tell each other
about wherever our lives seems to be taking us.
Though I've been stateside for six months, he points
towards Atlantic City's glowing pit and apologizes
that I must not have seen any of this in New Zealand,
but I explain to him that that country is not
without its machinery. Pipelines and water turbines,
hotel elevators and room lights. Though that island world
gushed with the wild, it too was scabbed
with foot-to-summit pulley rigs and frayed cables,
rusting cranes and generators. Though they no longer ran,
I knew how those engines would shudder and grunt,
what they call a haven of sin and slavery here,
they call a paradise elsewhere. In one language, an ice flow
is called *Ka Roimata o Hinehukatere*, in honor of a Maori
maiden's fallen lover, and in another it's the *Franz Josef Glacier*
for the way it recalls a dead Austro-Hungarian emperor's
muttonchops. The motorways and town names,
the lexicon, at times, so close to translation,
at others, unexplainable. My brother tells me again

that our mother is drifting further and further into herself.
He says she doesn't like how we don't talk much—
him and I—but we're on different schedules.
And when we say a night out, away from the family,
when we decide to change the subject to anything else,
we understand there is nothing between us
to say at all, so I cross over to the beach reeds
beside the boardwalk and pull two thin laths
out of the cheap dune fence, pass one to him and begin
our age old way of communicating, hitting each other,
laughing like lunatics. This is what we've always done,
our own language since childhood—the crack
of the planks on our skin, the welts on our arms
slowly emerging like driftwood breaking
the ocean's surface in the outgoing tide.

[○]

It is an art I can only fake—how I prune pine boughs
off the neighbor's tree bending further and further over
our fence each year, weave the clippings and tie ribbon
into Christmas grave blankets for my great-grandparents,
my grandmother. But, abroad again, I understand
something new about beliefs. If lightning struck an oak
and the jolted limb fell off the trunk, over the property line
and into my Jersey yard, my father would be the one
to clean up the wrecked foliage. If it fell on the other side,
there would be another father to gather the pieces.
But here—Ireland, Scotland, England—there are hedge walls
staking borders and between them, a man's arm span;
the fairy lane, a liminal space for the otherworldly.
Among these holy grounds, where spirits bury sacred tokens,
there is no easy way to disturb, no welcomed admission.
If you must enter, you must have offerings. Whenever I
return home, there are souvenirs, photographs,
and I have to hope these little gifts will convey the grace,
the memories and familial influence I carry everywhere I go.
The guilt one acquires in Catholic school lectures
isn't readily forgotten. When I tramped Croagh Patrick—
the mountain where the saint fasted for forty days and nights—
I ascended the craggy face barefoot, the true pilgrim's way,
not out of sin or fear, but some strange mix of faith
and reverence. When I nursed my blistered and bleeding feet,
I mended a barely-a-martyr's mark. Another time,
in New Zealand, soaked from the storm-soggy duff, I kept
my eye on Mitre Peak, shored each step through fallen, dew-
slick trunks like a trapeze artist, the mud swelling ankle deep.
Everything foundered into muck whole, including my left shoe
under a wrong step, and when I reached in to salvage it,
I plucked a silver butter knife sunken for forty years.

This was no little thing. More of what I've learned:
on any wandering, your feet must constantly test the ground;
if the earth hands you anything, you are on divinity's stoop.
At the cemetery, I walked around each plot, careful not to step
overtop of a body—a superstitious tick, I know, but can't help—
and genuflected before my grandmother's carved stone,
prayed my tribute might make up for what the dead
make possible, her heirlooms that found their way to me:
her father's ring, her Wheaton Glass bottle collection,
a plastic suitcase from the seventies—the one I use
on every trip, the one in which she wrote my name.

[○]

On the Bus-Eireann through Galway City center
heading out of town, studying street names
and one ways, I catch a sign for the Latin Quarter
and imagine my father's comment, "If only it was
just a quarter of the city." The Hispanic population
booming in my hometown of Vineland,
migrant workers trucked in each season to harvest
the fields. The Italian descendants do the hiring
and keep a keen eye on everyone like a careful parent.
These rivalries exist in every homeland. Mynondog,
an old Scot king, knew his kingdom and country
would long be disturbed by Anglo-Saxon invaders,
foresaw the unicorn of his descendants' crest
chained by the crown of the lion. Around London,
I couldn't help but notice the victor's seal everywhere.
The horned steed facing its captor. The brutish feline.
When England first colonized New Zealand,
they imported stoats and weasels to counter
the brush-birds, killed off dozens of species the world
had never seen, will never see again. Laughing Owl.
Huia. Stephens Island Wren. During the conquest
of Ireland, British "planters" worked the land
as much as the native tongue, named what
had already housed generations. The country paled:
Castledawson, Upperlands—the endless argument
of Londonderry or Derry. When I called home
yesterday, my sister told me that my brother
and father were rallied to an accident scene.
Some *goddamned illegal* ran a stop sign and slammed
into the side of a passenger car, a woman and her son
who I went to school with, who suffered
from *Osteogenesis imperfecta*—brittle bone disease—

had all his limbs broken on impact. My stomach
dropped, and I heard my mother ask my sister to do
another load of laundry, to put dinner in the oven
before she left for work, to tell me to call back,
that she's too tired to speak right now. I'm jarred back
to the bus when some drunk gets on and yells,
"What am I, black?" to the woman next him who doesn't
appreciate his advances. He grunts again,
"You fuckin' Polish are only good for scraping shit off a dirty plate."
And though the driver throws him off,
the damage is done. I hope the majority of those
on board don't agree with him. I hope my sister
can remember a time when our mother was good
at something, when people didn't break so easily.

[∘]

I have been here for months and still
there is something new, something else
that unsettles me. First, the scores
of eighteen year olds, piss-drunk
and pawing at each other, groping
and urinating in the street. Now,
the armed soldiers escorting bank vans
to each branch. According to gossip at the pub,
an IRA sect was found in town and local
enforcement expects the worst.
There seems to always be answers
at the bar. Just a week ago, after I had
returned from a week in Dublin, I finally
found someone to explain The Spire—
that huge spike—erected on O'Connell Street.
Nineteen sixty-six, the IRA blew up
the Nelson Pillar, another English marker
on foreign soil, and to replace it, the country
commissioned a national monument be built
in its place. In Galway, along the coast road,
marble statuaries recount Irish peasants
fleeing the famine. There is pride
in their ruin. There is nothing more
dangerous than a narrow love
for one's nation. Each year, I hear of another
friend gone abroad, escaping the rigid
Americas for a European worldview.
Each year, a friend or a friend of a friend
ends up paying some price—arm, leg,
life—in some branch of the military.
Each year, my mother writes me a letter
and this one is no different, no matter

if I'm off the continent. She pens
that she's worried, explains that I'm wiping
the family out of my life. On the isolated
plot of our home, there is no talking
with someone, only talking behind them.
In the Republic of Ireland, there is
traditional music and dancing, the national
ideal, a united island—preservation
of Irish heritage, making up perhaps for the six
lost counties, trying to feel whole. Every act
of violence, whether from one side
or the other, only serves
to make the border more futile.
Maori invasions and European diseases
and the Moriori people of the Chatham
Islands were decimated; the last,
full-blooded tribesman died
in nineteen thirty-three. The fight
to keep everyone united is more than
an uphill battle. Some would say
it's impossible, but it doesn't keep those
from trying. Not the military
from their beat to halt the unionists.
Not the modern day guerillas gumming up
the republic's works. Not the menacing pin,
pointed at the heavens, threatening to burst
its starlit rapture if ever it fell on them.

[○]

By the very nature of a trip, there is a departure
and a return. On my packing list, I've implemented
the slow marking off, the clean text of what I still need
to fold and stuff into my luggage. One piece at a time.
Attentive and sure that I haven't misplaced anything.
The littlest item lost always causes the biggest stir—
in New Zealand, if I climbed a peak and packed a lunch,
then I tramped out of the bush with my apple cores
and bread crumbs, worried of any foreign introduction
I might make. No Pink Lady groves amid the gorse.
No plum speckled between the cabbage palms.
Just fear to keep brush from being ruined with fruit trees.
Park law, a nice try at gathering what has already spoiled,
but still I can understand the effort. Whole forests
leveled on Easter Island: the tribal people needed trunks
to roll their huge, carved stone moai. In a few
generations, there was nothing left, no way to leave
their isle prison, no other home for which they could
set sail. My parents, my sister and brother ask me
how long I'll be *home*, before I take off again. The fact
that I haven't left the island, left Europe, and still
I need to decide on my next stop. No direction,
no bearing. After every place I travel to, I cross out
where I've been—*X* doesn't always mark the spot,
just a spent treasure. The only things I'm certain of
are the few things I've collected: a handful of rocks,
sea glass, a random spoon abandoned on the sidewalk.
Before there was ever any compass or astrolabe, ferries
or cargo ships, there was a young warrior and his kin
in their canoes, tribal clans, whole armies rowing,
faring the waves, drowning or arriving on a foreign shore.
No way any of us this day and age can comprehend
that ignorant spirit, that nerve and strange hope
for what lies out beyond the known, for no certain end.

PART III

DEFENDING THE ENTRANCE TO THE HEREAFTER

A BRIDGE IS LIKE A TONGUE

This night and nothing to say to anyone in the bar.
No one I quite know, so I poke at the ring of water
on the countertop left from my bourbon and club soda,
revisit again what my father said and how he said it—
"The bridges in Rhode Island are shit. Worst out there.
Watch it." A warning worth his telling. Something he read
in the daily or pieced together from an evening news clip.
I'm in the Ocean State and watching my fiancé
usher beers from waist-high fridges to the waitress station,
small talk and chit chat with patrons she grew up with,
old babysitters and neighbors, an occasional wink
in my direction. Introductions: *I'm the guy* and *Lucky indeed*.
In a booth by the front door, John sounds like he's talking
about the trouble I have with his accent—*a hard time*,
the phrase battered by the mortar and pestle of his drawl—
but, in actuality, commenting on his most recent
work assignment, to gold plate wisdom teeth for a woman.
Vinny, at his six-top table, is buying drinks for his mistress
and yelling about how he'd like to *Melt the bitch down*.
Bitch being his wife or an office building, though
I'm not sure which one or why. After my future
mother-in-law acquaints me with the Pawtucket Fire Chief,
the Hi-Lo Jack league, Jocko, Kathy, and Bobby, I settle up
my empty glass with a full one and meet Gary Moreau.

And because Gary is at this bar, I expect every other type
of story I have heard—corvette dealer, spring water
bottler, chef, factory worker of the plastic piece inside
soda bottle caps—but wind up with something I can
barely understand. Actually. Physically. I first assume
he's mentally disabled—and this may be terrible
that I make this mistake—but he can barely talk.
Most days I reconsider the people I talk to—the know-it-alls,
narcissists, and gabbers I usually attract. On more than one
occasion I have followed the stuttering tongue to revelation.

Those morning hours after the bar closed—tables wiped,
glasses emptied—I sat and waited for my fiancé to lock up
and asked for another drink when I shouldn't have.
My legs struggled to heave my trunk and my voice
lost its quick, sharp edge. Living is reason enough
for storytelling, introductions, and drinks. There are always
parts to observe and measure, like with the bridge,
suspension cables bolted and strung tower to tower
as if it were a jaw of pearly whites, abutments pinned to bed-
rock. A bridge is a tongue and, like the ones rotting
in the salt air of Rhode Island, Gary—a Vietnam vet—
was cornered on his walk home, beaten in an alley
off North Charles Street, suffered a stroke three days after
and though he relearned to ply a pool cue like a writer
guides a pen, though he practiced operating his mouth,
the muscles were structurally deficient. As usual,
I kept quiet, agreed and took note of what people said
in the booths behind me. John conceded that he
wasn't troubled with plating the enamel, the task of molding
a loop off the molars' roots—so she could wear them
around her neck—but with the woman. The *hard time*

was her story; his accent not simply the drawl, but the crack
in his voice. All she had left was his teeth: her son
was a random outlier, casualty, a tourist swallowed in jet fuel
and the crumpled steel of the Twin Towers. The *Bitch*
was, in fact, Vinny's wife and though he quickly changed
the subject to the quesadilla he was going to microwave
and eat when he got home, he did say he could
never thank her enough for his children. These nights
I remember all the things that fail us just when we need them
and forget there is no way to tell my almost-wife how
much I love her. *Watch your driving. Last thing I need is you
winding up dead*, my father's final plea still ringing, so I pass
the keys over and take the passenger seat, my breath
warming my fiancé's cold, work-sored hands
while the heater in her car won't kick on for the life of us.

THE SAME IDEA

Consider the principle of unvarying
validity, a law of constants: the ocean
tides, patterns of constellations, nights
of your childhood filled with burning,
no matter the season, and how they

stretch into now, to this holiday.
And though you are not one of the kids
chasing their fire-traced shadows
around the farm—finally one
of the adults—there is still the cadence

of semis grunting along Union Road,
the thorny drainage ditches
and mangled guardrails, ankles waiting
to be twisted in the deep plow rows
of the field the Christmas bonfire

has been kindled in. Year after year.
The farmers' mothers and teenage
liquor store cashiers, hairdressers
and linemen who spend days
above ground on phone poles,

the unemployed and overworked,
all exalting the only spirit they believe in,
one they can swallow, nips of liquor.
Plastic lawn chairs cast onto the pyre
sagging to a tarlike pool

around the glaring coals.
The flames still sing to you like gravel
under a tire tread, like the echoing
crackle of antlers. This religion
you return to, each time you're home,

is a sermon of wounds and sweat,
a practice of downing a shot
like you've already lost it. Beer cans,
windblown to the road,
clang like the license plates

of tow trailers scraping asphalt
as they leave town, the ones
you stare off and follow across
the black horizon, their passing by
only underscoring each short stay.

HOUNDS

It isn't just the fourth beer sinking in, or drizzle's static
sounding through the porch screen, but the soggy rot
wafting from the ash tree crumbling into itself, pulled out
root to limb—all of it carries memory to the foot

of my stoop. Some tenant must have phoned the landlady,
worried the trunk might topple onto a sedan's hood,
crush a toddler, but—whatever the case—the moldy whiff
reminds me of wet dog: first, my rowdy mutt, Ernie,

who hooked his collar on the top hinge of his crate
and choked overnight, the one I woke up early to feed
and stared at until my mother found me, snatched me off
to her bed throwing the covers over me while she called

my father at work to ask him what part of the field
she should bury him in, where the shovel was; and second,
my friend's gray-whiskered and starved beagle, a July Fourth
cookout not ruined, but quieted by rain.

Coolers of beer brimming though everyone had stumbled
to bed hours ago, all except me and the dog and Steve.
Bottle after bottle. We dug past the thick top layer of ice
to the colder ones underneath, the dog, Cassie, tonguing

and chewing on the cubes we tossed her from the chest,
and when we went for our third pass at the spread
on the picnic table, filling plates with cold burgers, beans,
coleslaw and honeydew slices, she wanted some, too.

She nuzzled at my feet, snapped and whimpered for a bite,
and when I wouldn't scrape over anything, she went to Steve.
Midchew, he noticed Cassie and spit a beef chunk
onto the patio floor. She swallowed it and then

looked up at him as if to beg for more. Ambrosia salad.
Ketchup-slicked French fries. But when Cassie
wouldn't eat a tomato slice, the wad of pickle relish
on his boot, Steve shouted, "Finish your vegetables,"

and swung his hard palm against her flanks; Steve, who once
told me his father made him shoot his own dog
when he was eight. Steve, who mercy killed a hawk,
broke its neck after it soared into his car and paralyzed itself,

washing the blood from his hands in the January chill
of the Jersey Atlantic. Steve, on the country's holiday—
having forgotten, maybe, that I was even there—
who gripped and wrestled Cassie's snout into the mess

on the ground, swatted at her jowls and hollered, "Eat up.
You better take it," punching, yelling, but then broke off.
He must have surprised himself with his own violence,
but then again, maybe he only remembered I was there.

Maybe there is no measure for how the human mind
can react, no way to predict its wants and failings.

Wires crossed. Misfires. But in this moment, there is only
a man and a dog, stash of dwindling drinks, smattering of food

pieces on a porch. Steve Pait, who suffered POW training
and was taught by the army how the enemy would treat him,
who, for weeks, sleeplessly huddled in his "prison" coop—
barely a day's rations, hard labor—who was forced to shuffle

in muck for hours, ordered to chant "Boots" with each step,
but repeated "Boobs" as a little mutiny to keep sane. Steve,
who picked bar brawls, whom I remember best for practicing
how to pass the hollow IV needle through the soft flesh

of his arm on his weekend off from medic drills at Ft. Bragg,
leaning over my kitchen counter, slowly losing accuracy
with each bottle of Icehouse he threw back.
The thin purl of blood faintly stained the counter

no matter how much bleach I used, but that July holiday
is too far from that strange game of doctor,
and that Independence Day cookout too distant for me
to recollect, perfectly, what Steve was like that night,

how rough he really was, how many beers he had,
how I sat on the lawn chair. Every July before this one,
I picked the liquor cabinet clean, lit bottle rockets and tossed
firecrackers at trucks gunning down the county road,

stumbled behind the shed to piss, saw the day as nothing
more than a reason to get blitzed and listen to my grandfather
who never failed to stand straighter when the National Anthem
played. I forgot my hand-over-heart once, and learned

my lesson. It would take a draft order, a boot sole
dug into my lower back every day of recruit exercises,
air raids, and mines off the ship's bow for me to even grasp
what my grandfather was shoved into; one of three in his class

to come back alive. And it would take an order, day before
the Fourth of July, with your deployment date and how long
you'd man the frontline for me to want to drink and drain a cooler
into the night, curse and shout and hit a hungry, panting hound.

And it would take a strange impulse to shroud your son
in bed sheets—albeit a misguided, loving one—while you
took spade to clay and carved a hole deep enough
for you to bury a dog. Steve Pait, wracked with something

I can't begin to know in that moment, on that screened porch,
then cradled the beagle, Cassie, to his leg, softly now, petting,
scratching her neck, gave her his plate of crumbs and grease,
and leaned down and whispered to her, a soft mumble

I will never know. Much of my life I have been a witness
to things I cannot understand or can only half remember
how it was, can only remember the characters of the story,
not how it ended. But this is a lucky occasion,

this evening with the rain outside the door,
having moved onto my fifth beer, the stink of soaked canine
thick in my kitchen, spectator to the rotting
and these moments flooding back: when my mother

pulled back the comforter and held me, gently ran her fingernails
across my scalp, the scent of strawberry hand soap

still fresh on her skin; when I staggered to sleep before Steve,
and—nearly passed out—watched as he went back

to the sliding glass door and let Cassie in from her patio pen,
shouldered the dog to his air mattress, hunkered down
for the hangover that holiday always seemed to attract. Tonight,
branches snap in the rain, and I wonder under which droplet.

ON GARAGES

Somehow, I've wound up here, curtained in a cool, late summer's
      midnight, breaking into a neighbor's garage through
the unlocked window, not drunk or stoned, but bored
      and ballsy-curious, rummaging through the tool chest
and refrigerator—batteries in the butter tray, leftover cake
      between two paper plates wrapped in green cellophane,
a long-neck old enough for the label to have peeled itself off—
      everything measured and the symmetry alien,
clean cut and categorized so I can't understand. How odd
      and expected it is when I remember what a garage
is supposed to look like, as if a postal worker who happens upon
      a picture of the human heart on the cover of a magazine
he's delivering, the beads of veins on the lumpy muscle,
      purple and red and white, must think to himself, "Yes,
that's correct. That's inside me," not the inked symbol one sees
      too often on greeting cards, but the actual heart,
like the neat shelves and hooks with ladders and tree pruners
      in this garage, the floor as carefully swept and organized
as an operating room. I had only known the unfortunate,
      cruddy wrecks of wire spools and mismatched cans
of dried paint, queer cuts and nubs of lumber, plumb bobs
      without strings, drawers of sockets all the same size,
a man cursing as he snakes between cardboard boxes bent in
      and busted at the bottom seam, as he digs for

the blunt-tip of the linesman's pliers somewhere in a sea
　　　　of tarps and empty oil cans, a man who exhales
his plans of structure and harmony for the space out loud:
　　　　"Bolt a countertop below the electric panel. Assemble
a wall of nooks where power tools can fit, label it. Buy
　　　　a new thirty-pack for the minifridge," as if reciting a prayer—
the incense of gear grease thick in the cramped tool house.
　　　　The clutter and jumble I once knew as the mark of someone
engrossed in his own life, of someone observing a physical landscape
　　　　he can create and scale, build and pare back, architect,
candlemaker, a weekend ranger pruning the shrubs in his front yard.
　　　　No butcher or airplane pilot. No slob, but a fanatic.
A tomcat crouched on the hatch of a sewer drain, protective,
　　　　as if the bunker it defended were an entrance
to the hereafter. A man whose sanctuary has no room for cars.

LETTER ABOUT MY LAST NIGHT
IN CARBONDALE, ILLINOIS

To Colin Joseph Campbell

Though we haven't talked in over a month, you must
know I am moving again—three years crammed into my
hatchback and the bed of my father's truck—and though he
and my sister have driven out to help, this is no easy task.
Just as a single water glass always seems to shatter, despite
the ginger handling and wrapping, ruining the even set, so too
was my last night in Carbondale settled with something for
which I couldn't prepare.

Crossing town to donate my writing desk and random
knickknacks, I didn't realize the thrift store parking lot was glazed
with black ice until I skidded and faced an adjacent parking lot,
a rig's cargo trailer, and what looked like a homeless man
wintering beneath.

He flailed his cane in my headlights, yelling, and after
I decided it wasn't because I woke him up, I tiptoed across
the frozen asphalt. He was fine despite his left foot twisted
toward the opposite direction. And when he asked me to feel
if anything was broken, that is when I thought of you and didn't

think any alternative existed, that there was no other option
but to kneel and cup my hands around his bony, splintered joint.

Do you know what a snapped leg feels like? The best
I can compare it to is that of a twig's broken end poking
through the rubber skin of a balloon. He quietly grabbed my
hand (which I didn't notice until he spoke again), and when he
said it had been hours, that he was numb between his ankle
and hip, I didn't care if you aren't supposed to move someone,
gripped him under his armpits and dragged him out. This isn't
the first time I've ignored warnings. All I wanted was to look him
in the eyes because, because when I need to calm someone,
I need to believe there isn't a problem.

Feel a broken bone, and believe it's all right. Pack a car,
and believe you haven't missed something and get on
with the long, tiring drive.

At the same moment I tried to ease Lloyd—the name
of the man, I found out while on the phone with the 911 operator—
I wanted to stop waiting on hold for the medics to arrive, and call
my father and sister who had probably fallen asleep waiting for me
to drop off furniture and pick up the pizzas we'd ordered. To call
you and ask if you thought he overcompensated for the heavy basket
wire-tied to the back of his ten speed, caused the rear tire to fishtail,
and dropped him on his left knee? I only ask because you seem
to know these types of things. You've lifted my car off of a brick
embankment with little more than a cheap jack and door stoppers.

While the sirens chipped away at the windless cold, one EMT
by Lloyd's shoulders, one—with a lip of chew—by his calves,
I manned the crippled kneecap and we lifted him, screaming,

onto the stretcher. If you asked me in that moment, I couldn't say
what was left for me to pack when I got back to the apartment,
if I really needed to keep the four plates, four bowls, and three glasses
wrapped in newspaper and ready for the trip east.

Please excuse me, I'm forgetting myself, I meant to tell you
what Lloyd made me promise: he was so worried about his bike,
the Tupperware of leftovers, the ream of paper, stuffed animals
and Christmas lights wrapped around the top tube, that he wanted
me to deliver the mess to his house. Between his calls of pain
came exact directions, the name of someone I was supposed to find
(a "Sean," but I don't know if I spelled that right).

Before I knew it, the bike was jammed into my small
hatchback, and I was in front of his slumping porch, cling wrap
over the windows, flashing holiday bulbs—his directions were
amazingly perfect—you too wouldn't have stopped, but fulfilled
Lloyd's request, like the Patron Saint of Close Calls, Freak Accidents,
and Happenstance. Sean (still, I'm not sure of the spelling) was so
horrified to hear of his friend's predicament that he pushed past
and waited for me to unlock the passenger door.

Colin, I want to tell you about the fisherman's hook
on his hat brim. I want to tell you about the small talk we shared on
the short drive to understand what Lloyd had gone through, but it is
impossible. It is beyond language. The pizza is cold and both my
father and sister are asleep at the apartment.

What about me? All I had given away was a few accessories
and some kitchenware, the rest all bundled and stuffed into my car
and the bed of my father's truck. Yes, there is a virtue in packing light—
jettisoning the rest—but there is also an awareness in what you truly

need that I'm afraid I will never have. Pray for me on this one. There
are still boxes to tape closed at the apartment. Still time to empty them.

What if I hadn't driven to the thrift store to give away
my furniture? And what if Lloyd lay there all night? What if I was too
freaked or tired or hungry to walk across the parking lot to see
what he wanted? And though I had my reservations about the whole
thing, I still couldn't help but help.

I don't know if this is a comment on the world, humanity,
or morality, but maybe you can help me with the idea. This letter
is already too long. You always seem to say things simply. Another
flaw to put on my list. Is a fault nothing more than a motive for our
existence? Our ability to aid, a by-product of our condition? Damn,
I sure do wax poetic—like the bottom seam of a cardboard box
giving out, the contents crashing over the sidewalk—when all I want
is someone to tell me something straight. There. That's it. I've said it.

SEVEN PLACES I HAVE FOUND MY GRANDMOTHER IN THE LAST SIX YEARS

I)   The last place, Veteran's Cemetery of Cumberland County, Bridgeton, NJ: All it did was pour. I figured the purple button-up and matching necktie were appropriate because she thought it so dapper on me at my cousin's wedding—I hadn't worn it since. Got mud on my suitpant legs, though I tried not to. The whole time I kept thinking in words, something like a prayer, or something I would have said to her, my apology, an "Is it too late?" What I wanted to say was, "I am sorry I forgot to call you on your birthday," but everyone must have one of these regrets. At least I could have sent a card. *I'm sorry. I'm sorry.* We put her in the ground and her friends walked down the line, soaking wet, and kept saying, "I'm sorry." Right now, all I want to remember is the color of the dress she was buried in.

II)   On an airplane, from Raleigh-Durham International Airport to Philadelphia International Airport: I guess she was prepping the drink trolley in the back of the cabin, and I usually sit as close to the front as possible, but when she came up to deliver the preflight talk—complete with tools for demonstrating the safety features of the Boeing 737 I would be flying on—I was happy to see her finally getting out and seeing the world. Her odd build in the airline's uniform. Her rolling eyes and half-hearted smile. Those last years, she was plugged into a dialysis machine, so it's nice to have her making up for lost time. *To undo the buckle, lift the latch. To start the flow of oxygen, firmly pull down on the mask.* She knew well the value in both of these. After I finished my in-air Bloody Mary, I was sure it was she, when she got me another one free of charge.

III) In a dream (1), my college apartment, fall semester of my junior year, Burlington, North Carolina: It's nighttime at my grandparents' old house on Chestnut Avenue, and outside, the Jane magnolia not in bloom, the zoysiagrass soft under foot (or maybe I am confusing this memory with my brain actually processing my jersey sheets), in the front yard, my grandmother is crying and trying to get away from my grandfather, but when he moves he bounds, speeds by, unfathomably quick. And when he finally stands stock still, he is enraged, breathing in deep breaths, staring at me. He almost looks like he wants to cry. I lose track of my grandmother and for a brief moment forget she was even there.

IV) In a smell, Union Hotel & Restaurant, Greymouth, South Island, New Zealand: I want to pinpoint it. What was it? The scoop of garlic butter melting on the cheap steak? The escarole in the soup? Someone's flatulence? Dust? The faint smell of pinecones dipped in candle wax? She used to have this lotion—like the Avon kind, except the company was called Melaleuca (I'll never forget that word, I don't think)—with eucalyptus. Maybe that's it. I was using a eucalyptus leaf as a bookmark in my copy of *Ishmael*. Or maybe the water stain and mold on the pages' edges? Like her used edition of Longfellow's *Song of Hiawatha*. Maybe a fresh bar of Ivory soap? Or maybe pool water? Chopped celery? Dry-rotted couch cushions?

V) At the Catholic Social Services building, on the corner of US-51S, Carbondale, Illinois: Out the passenger window—her name on the cornerstone of a two-story brick office; alight on the dogwood beside the road, a cardinal. That's it, but I think this is enough to say she was there.

VI) In Taaffe's Public House, Shop Street, Galway, Ireland: There must have been two-dozen bags of her clothes that we donated to the Salvation Army, but apparently she held on to her favorite, or else found another one somewhere over here—a dead ringer—and decided to show it off. Everyone has his or her bad habits, and I guess she picked up smoking, grabbed a pack of Marlboro Gold and a turquoise lighter from her jacket in the corner of the booth. She would have been furious if I walked out into this kind of cold without a coat on. But, I guess, at this point, there wasn't much that I could say that would change anything. When she came back from her smoke break, she sang, knew every traditional ballad, measure for measure, and ordered two Miller Genuine Draft bottles for herself. In each tune, every lyric, her voice crooned, there was her familiar pitch that I could and couldn't remember.

VII)   In a dream (2), on my parents' couch, sometime between *Ebert Presents* and *Daisy Cooks!*, Vineland, New Jersey: My grandmother is smoking a thin cigar—maybe a clove or Black and Mild—while she changes the sheets on her and my grandfather's separate twin beds. White sheets swapped for a chalky green set. She's wearing her housecoat and staring, in a way I don't ever remember her staring, at me—so, instead, I decide to sit with my grandfather in the living room while she cleans. And just as I leave the bedroom, her cigar ashes onto the linen and she sweeps it off with the back of her hand. She says, *It's okay. Really, it's fine. I'm just tired. Go, and I'll be out in a minute.*

CONVERSION

Forthill Cemetery, Galway, Ireland

Donnelly's fuel depot engines boom and catch the cemetery's walled atrium—whole family lines scribed on towering crosses, moss scrub bearding the block and headstones: remnants of an Augustinian fort shadowing the petrol station and Bord Na Móna banners wire-tied to fences spanning Lough Atalia road. The whiff of peat briquettes and patina on plaques beside the gate set a tone for the romantic, if only the markers didn't record the execution of three hundred Spanish sailors, nameless, interred on the site hundreds of years before the first crypts and gardened grave plots here, if only there wasn't the blade edges of shattered bottles cemented along the low ramparts and high grounds overlooking the oil distributor's roof. Here, conversion is unimaginable: how flesh gives itself to root, how plant beds fossilize into combustibles, how foot lanes emerge and vanish within steps from where they start and chiseled mortuary slabs are unwritten from weathering. As unthinkable as the barred chapel serving as the groundskeeper's work shed, housing knots of a string trimmer's plastic cutting line, grease cans, crates of votive candles and rubber waders. Unbelievable, as the buried lot—softening into the earth—hearing the drumfire of conveyor belts, buffet of coal lumps in chutes above them, believing the whole world must be fighting to get in.

BLACKROCK DIVING TOWER

Salthill Promenade, Galway, Ireland

Concrete crumbles under the salt. Whole chunks
from the block bench, the changing locker,
exposing rebar underneath rusting into dust,
paint from the support poles holding up the rain eaves,
one layer at a time, color by color: red, orange, blue.

Graffiti chipped into the masonry is blotted away.
These steps molded onto the jetty—odd stairs,
promenade to ocean—are what we claim
and reclaim from the moving tide. Seaweed,
slicking everything, scraped from boat ramps,

ladder rungs, the diving boards, so swimmers
can ascend the tower without slipping
and break the water's surface beyond
the shallow shore ledge. Winter barely ebbed,
and in the rainy cold a man has come here and kicked

the wall for a safe return home. Another man
has shed his boots and walked into the kelp whorls,
waist high in the surf. A cormorant on the quay
tries to swallow a whole sand eel, bobbing its head back
to get the entire thing down its throat, inch

by fishy inch, but the meal cannot give to the small core
of its stomach. I don't understand how anyone
can move in this chilly water, especially this man here,
unflinching as he goes deeper and deeper.
Clouds barrel in as quickly as they go out. I stare

at the curtain of showers being pulled one side
of the mountains to the other, and when I turn back,
he's disappeared, dashed into the waves. It won't
be long before the briny tang will be washed
from my heavy coat, won't be long before his next breath.

TURKEY POINT

For my father and grandfather

We're two hours too late for the tide,
the ribs of boat hulls already breaking
the channel's thinning current, the purling

vein of tea-colored water lipping the silt
shore and dense sedge knotted with lost
bobbers and nets, fishing cords draped

from the walking bridge at the road's end,
the vanishing scribble of each stray line
in the puttering flow. The only catch

we've come out here for is catching up.
Maybe an odd blue claw in our ring traps
but doubtful, so we pay more attention

to the bait fisherman wading the shallows,
the slow draining of beer from our cans,
your father, my grandfather, sunning along

the bank—his legs tire too quickly to climb
the few stairs—or the purple martins
flitting over the back bay, darting to and from

their nests under the bridge eaves, circling
each other seamlessly. We have finally found
ourselves some time where I am home,

you off shift, your father sharp enough
for a day out. I say nothing about my life
outside of the state. Though the creek is only

a trickle, the fisherman cleaves crabs with a single
hatchet swing and tosses the split carapaces
into minnow baskets, the old, pecked shells

and pinchers pitched into marsh snares
for the gulls. *Take a look for yourself,* you say
and motion over to your father craning

to see us on the pedestrian deck, *Mornings
I come off shift, I check on him and he's sitting there
so quiet, I just don't know if he's still here.*

Weathered bulkheads and rotted duck blinds
grow from the bottom of the emptying pools,
graffiti written in mud now visible

on the arch's belly—Tia and Rich 4 Ever,
Fuck This Shit, Jersey Blows, Donnie '97—
the twilight, crisp and aged, lolls the wetland,

rallies the night-coming silence with din.
*Every phone call I get, I have to say to myself
he might be gone,* a pause as if you understand

what you're admitting, *but anyway, when are you*
heading back to Illinois? And what should I tell a son
who doesn't want to say goodbye to his father?

Cedar boughs and thicket are a blooming stroke,
a perch of fish bones. *Maybe Wednesday, but*
I can stay longer, though we both know everything

is in motion. You check the barren crab traps
in the briny bed and I look off to the dry reeds
crackling in the wind. The distance draws in

The falling dark is built in moon slats.

NOTES

"Bivalve, Cumberland County": This poem grew from the news article "Oysters, the Only Game in Bivalve" published in the April 11, 1992 issue of *The New York Times*.

"Burning Down the Camper": This poem owes a debt of gratitude to Andrew McFadyen-Ketchum.

"Jersey Devil": The legend of the Jersey Devil dates back to 1735 and is centered around Leeds Point, New Jersey. There are many variations to the story, but the simplest elements revolve around Mother Leeds giving birth to her thirteenth child, which she cursed to be a demon.

"Our Lady of Mount Carmel": The festival mentioned in this poem is the Our Lady of Mount Carmel Festival held in Hammonton, New Jersey. The festival's roots go back to 1875, when a group of Italian immigrants held a front-yard procession and prayer session to thank the Virgin Mary for safe passage to their new country.

"Palace Depression": This poem is based on a structure of the same name that at one time stood on Mill Road, just off of Landis Avenue, in Vineland, New Jersey. George Daynor—a self-proclaimed prophet and millionaire-turned-pauper-turned-architect—built a house from trash on a junkyard he bought for four dollars. The "Home of Junk" (as it was referred to) was opened on December 25, 1932 and was razed in 1969. It was created as a tribute to innovation and the human spirit, to show that people could overcome the Great Depression. I owe a debt of gratitude to the writers of the *Weird N.J.* book and *Raw Vision Magazine*, issue 7, as well as Sarah McCartt-Jackson for her keen eye and suggestions, especially in the second section. I would also like to mention that recent efforts by Jeff Tirante and

Kevin Kirchner are bringing new attention to the Palace Depression and painstakingly reimagining and reconstructing the castle from its ruins.

"So Intricate, So Inconceivably Complex": This title comes from a Nikola Tesla quote. In 1893 he noted, "A single ray of light from a distant star falling upon the eye of a tyrant in bygone times may have altered the course of his life, may have changed the destiny of nations, may have transformed the surface of the globe, so intricate, so inconceivably complex are the processes in Nature." The form of this poem owes a debt of gratitude to Philip Levine's "Facts." Lastly, "The Jitterbug" referenced in the seventh stanza refers to Betty Hutton's 1939 song recording, not Judy Garland's version that was deleted from the film *The Wizard of Oz.*

"Standing in the Atlantic Ocean with Tesla's Pigeon": The phrase "a morsel of cinder" is borrowed from Rumer Godden's translation of Carmen Bernos De Gasztold's poem "The Prayer of the Glowworm." The shore town where this poem takes place is Strathmere, with specific reference to the beach skirting the Corson's Inlet Bridge.

"Turkey Point": Turkey Point (located in Dividing Creek, New Jersey) is a local crabbing and minnow fishing spot. This poem, particularly the last line, owes a debt of gratitude to Sarah McCartt-Jackson.

ACKNOWLEDGMENTS

Many thanks to the editors of the following journals where poems in this book first appeared, sometimes in different versions:

Arroyo Literary Review, "On Garages"

Burnside Review, "A Bridge is like a Tongue"

Cave Wall, "Water was always the problem surrounding" (as "From The Island Meditations")

Cold Mountain Review, "The Pecking Order"

Columbia Poetry Review, "So Intricate, So Inconceivably Complex" (as "So Inconceivably Complex")

Connotation Press: An Online Artifact, "The Island Meditations"

Copper Nickel, "Field Lessons" and "Turkey Point"

Georgetown Review, "On Thunderstorms"

The Hollins Critic, "Conversion"

Iron Horse Literary Review, "On Peeling Skin"

Labletter, "Standing in the Atlantic Ocean with Tesla's Pigeon" and "Blackrock Diving Tower"

Los Angeles Review, "Jersey Devil"

Mason's Road, "Letter about My Last Night in Carbondale, Illinois"

Milk Money, "Bivalve, Cumberland County"

North American Review, "Scrap Iron"

The Pinch, "Seven Places I Have Found My Grandmother in the Last Six Years"

Poet Lore, "Midnight Shift"

Prairie Schooner, "Hounds" and "Working First Shift at the Progresso Soups Factory"

Quiddity, "Palace Depression"
South Carolina Review, "His Grandmother as a Wind Chime"
Southern Poetry Review, "Burning Down the Camper"
West Branch, "The Same Idea"
Yalobusha Review, "Our Lady of Mount Carmel"

Many thanks to my mentors and teachers: Kevin Boyle, Drew Perry, Tita Ramirez, Cassie Kircher, and Allison Joseph. I would also, especially, like to thank Rodney Jones and Judy Jordan, not just for their support and guidance, but their profound, tireless, and endless readings of my many poems—in some cases, the same ones (over and over and over again)—and, in particular, this manuscript. I am indebted to all of you for the after-class discussions and critiques, the opportunities, fried chicken, tofu, and beer.

I am also extremely grateful for receiving a research grant from the Irish Studies Department at Southern Illinois University Carbondale (SIUC), in conjunction with the National University of Ireland at Galway, which afforded me the opportunity to live, write, and work on this book in Ireland during the 2011 spring semester.

Many thanks to Kathleen Graber for selecting my book as winner of the 2012 Agha Shahid Ali Poetry Prize; her close read and attention to my manuscript has been incredible. Not to mention, my sincerest gratitude to Stephanie Warnick, Jessica Booth, Linda Manning, Glenda Cotter, and Kate Coles, as well as everyone else at the University of Utah Press for bringing this book to publication and treating it with such care and respect.

Thanks also to the following friends and writers who challenged me to be a better artist, observer, and human: Colin Campbell, Hunter Copeland, Kerry James and Renee Evans, Vince Farinaccio and the VF Players, Jillian Jackson and Bradford Krieger, Brenna Lemieux, Lou Magazzu, Kevin and Danielle Malone, Sarah McCartt-Jackson, Travis and Regina Mossotti, Matthew Spainhour, and all of my peers at SIUC.

All of the poems in this book have gotten this far because of the attention and careful reading my wife, Jessica Keough, has given them. The excitement and interest she has expressed for each of these works is, maybe, second to my own—on most days. On those others, when the whole blessed craft comes crashing down on me, she finds the time (despite work schedules and her own art making) to rally me back to a forgotten verse, a stanza I thought was never worth my time. I don't have the words, yet, to thank her for all that she has done—both for this collection and for me—but I plan on spending the rest of my life, reading, writing, and finding the lexicon to begin to tell her (in the most perfect way) how good she is and how, because of her efforts, I am a better thinker, friend, poet, husband, and person.

My parents, Mark and Dawn, afforded me a tremendous childhood and education, and for that I can never thank them enough. My sister and brother, Colby and Joey, have been incredible teachers and cohorts and their experiences, examples, and lessons will forever be a subject for amazement and reflection. To all of them, to my entire family, there is no way to express my truest, deepest gratitude for all that you have done, how you have helped me get to here, but I will try my best to figure it out.

This book is dedicated to my father, Mark Jay Brewin Sr., for the long hours he's spent at work, his companionship, and the example he has and always will set for me.